Henry Brown, Harriet Martineau, James Augustus Marshall

The Present and Future Prospects of Chicago

Henry Brown, Harriet Martineau, James Augustus Marshall

The Present and Future Prospects of Chicago

ISBN/EAN: 9783337425678

Printed in Europe, USA, Canada, Australia, Japan

Cover: Foto ©Suzi / pixelio.de

More available books at **www.hansebooks.com**

THE

Present and Future Prospects of Chicago:

AN ADDRESS

Delivered before The Chicago Lyceum,

January 20, 1846.

BY HENRY BROWN, ESQ.,
Author of "History of Illinois."

At a meeting of the Chicago Lyceum, held at the Court House, in the City of Chicago, on the evening of the 28th of January, ult. Mark Skinner, Esq., Vice-President in the Chair, and George Manierre, Secretary.

It was Resolved, That Henry Brown, Esq., President of said Lyceum, be requested to furnish a copy of his Inaugural Address for publication, and that Dr. Wm. B. Egan, Mr. Wm. M. Larrabee, and Mr. Thomas Hoyne be appointed a Committee to superintend its publication.

MARK SKINNER, *Vice-President.*
George Manierre, *Secretary.*

CHICAGO:
FERGUS PRINTING COMPANY,
244-8 ILLINOIS STREET.
1876.

INAUGURAL ADDRESS.

GENTLEMEN OF THE LYCEUM:— In entering upon the duties assigned me, as President of this Lyceum, I shall at present do little more than thank you for the honor conferred upon me by the appointment, and assure you in the simplicity of my heart, as every militia officer does in New England, from the General of Brigade, down to the Fourth Corporal, on his elevation "to rank and fame," that "I will endeavor to serve you according to the best of my abilities."

In order, however, that I may do so, it is necessary that I speak to you with freedom. This I shall do at all events, both now and hereafter, whether you hear or whether you forbear.

Our Saviour while on earth, in speaking to those he addressed, said they were a generation of vipers, that they were wolves in sheep's clothing, and so forth. The Apostle Paul used language equally plain and often as severe. The elder Cato, in speaking of the Roman people, said, "They were like sheep, for as those can scarcely be brought to stir singly, but all in a body readily follow their leaders;" just such are ye. "The men whose council you would not take as individuals, lead you with ease in a crowd." It may, perhaps, be so with us, and, to a certain extent, it unquestionably is.

It is not, however, my intention to speak thus of you or of this people; because it would give offence, and I am unwilling, especially on this occasion, to say anything which can by possibility be tortured into disrespect, and so long as it shall be my fortune, good or ill, to preside over this

Institution, I hope and trust that nothing will be said in discussion here, or even attempted, which ought to offend the most delicate ear. It is better for us, gentlemen, situated as we are, and living in a singular age, to imitate the forbearance of a distinguished clergyman, who being invited to preach before the Royal Court of France, in a by-gone age, at the conclusion of a thrilling discourse, told them if they did not do so and so, they would go to a place he forbore to mention in that courtly audience. While the oak, whose sturdy arms resist the tempest, is uptorn by its roots—the pliant reed, that yields to the blast, escapes unhurt. The human tongue, as Plutarch expresses it, "accustomed to speak with freedom in the cause of Justice," is an instrument of great power. It is the lever of Archimedes that moves the moral world. With truth for its support it is irresistible. The most stupid and exalted of our race obey its impulse and feel its power. How important then that its use be cultivated, and its efforts be aright directed. Such, gentlemen, is in part our object in coming hither, and so long as we adhere to such intentions, so long we shall deserve and without doubt meet with public approbation.

In order, gentlemen, that our efforts may be useful, an addition to our number will be necessary. A learned divine, on being told by one of his parishioners that he had thought for sometime of joining the church, knowing the applicant to be unworthy, informed him that the church was full; and that they had pretty much concluded not to take any more. It is not so, gentlemen, with us. The Lyceum is not yet full, we shall therefore be happy to receive additions, provided the applicants be worthy. We wish, however, to have it understood that admission here are not of course. The wisdom of ancient Persia has frequently been extolled. In her renowned Capitol there was, as we are informed, in olden times, an institution in some respects like ours. The number of its members, however, was limited; and being very select, the learned, and the wise, the patriot, the hero, and the sage, the most distinguished courtiers, and the most accomplished scholars in the realm sought and obtained admission thither. As a perpetual memento that its numbers were thus limited, and in no event whatever to be increased, a vessel filled with water to the brim, so that a single drop additional would cause it to overflow, was placed beside the chair;

around it were vases of the choicest flowers, whose fragrance filled the apartment, and whose beauty delighted every eye; at the time of which I speak, there was, we are told, in Persia's Capitol, a youth of rare attainments. His mind just then emerging into manhood, was the delight of Persia's Court; the Prince saw him and was charmed, the courtier, the scholar, and the statesman were all delighted, and with one accord desired that he, against their rules, might be admitted among their number. He was accordingly invited to attend their meetings, and a request at last to be admitted was preferred. It was seconded by the Prime Minister of the great King, but the President, pointing to the vessel, then before him, already full, the motion was withdrawn. The youth, however, still persisting, and in his zeal, forgetting where he was, with a step lighter than any fairy, advanced towards the chair, and plucking from the choicest flower the vase contained, a rose-leaf of surpassing beauty, he placed it with gentle hand upon the surface of the sparkling element, where it floated a monument of his triumph, without causing a drop to overflow. I need not inform you, gentlemen, that he was at once admitted by acclamation. I mention this not with a view to induce the gay world to join us, and thus contribute a little to our library, our funds, and to our moral and intellectual capital, but to show that perseverance is all-powerful, and that by proper efforts, the case of those as yet excluded from our number, and the enjoyment of privileges which ought to be highly valued, is not entirely hopeless.

Since the establishment of this Lyceum in 1834, I have been invited frequently to speak before it. I was invited so to do early in 1837, and chose for my theme "The present and future prospects of Chicago." My remarks, however, though well-intended, were by some unkindly taken. The speculation then in vogue, by which so many had been enriched, was not commended quite so highly as many supposed it ought. Besides, some doubts were then expressed, whether the system would endure, and whether speculation, with neither industry nor economy to aid it, would exalt us as a people. I then supposed, and still suppose, as Shakespeare says, that—

> "He's a bad surgeon, who for pity spares
> The part infected, till the gangrene spreads,
> And all the body perishes."

The Lyceum then was held in a dilapidated building on Clark street, between Ogden's Building and the Sherman House alley, used as a church; a building which led a stranger, as we are told, when passing through Chicago, to remark, "That he had frequently heard of God's house, but never saw His barn before." Our circumstances since, have somewhat changed; some sixteen, seventeen, or eighteen churches, vying in splendor with houses of public worship in the Atlantic cities, now stand triumphantly before us as mementos of piety and the arts, nowhere in towns of equal magnitude scarcely equalled, certainly in none excelled.

We are permitted also to hold our meetings in a Court House, erected on public credit, and to our shame be it spoken, wherein the prospect of its redemption is distant and uncertain.

On the 16th of June, 1831, twenty-four lots in the City of Chicago, given by the United States, among other lands, to the State of Illinois, for the use of the Illinois and Michigan Canal, were granted by letters patent, bearing date on that day, and executed by the Governor, to the County of Cook, "to aid said County in the erection of public buildings, and to the use and for the purposes before mentioned." I quote from the deed of trust, which is on record here. The lots in question are among the most valuable in Chicago; six of them are upon Lake street, and five upon Water street. Of the twenty-four lots thus patented, sixteen have been sold, worth at the present time $100,000, not for the purpose of erecting public buildings, but to pay current expenses. The remaining eight are yet unsold, and constitute what is called the Public Square, the block on which we now are assembled. Whether the State erred or not, in making the grant, I will not pause to enquire. The County of Cook being the grantor, and interested in the trust, it behooves us not to scrutinize the act too closely. Inasmuch, however, as it has been proposed to sell the public square, not for the purpose of erecting public buildings and executing thus the trust, but for the purpose of paying the County debt, prodigally contracted, a few remarks upon the subject seem now appropriate.

It is needless here to say that such an act would be an act of double treachery, because it is to all apparent, though men often "love the treason who despise the traitor." A deed like this would not, I apprehend, be sanctioned or approved. Reserved for public use. and embellished as it ought to be, with trees and shrubbery, it will be an ornament to our City, and generations now unborn will yet arise and bless us for having spared it.

But to resume the subject from which I have thus digressed. In 1842, I was again requested to address this Lyceum, I chose on that occasion for my theme again the subject for which I had been abused, the (then) present and future prospects of Chicago, and promised in my discourse to resume the subject five years thereafter. That time has not arrived, I am, however, requested to anticipate a little, and redeem a promise which has a year to run. Expecting, as I do, a discount on the debt for paying in advance. I undertake the task with pleasure, and will endeavor to discharge its duties without fear, favor, or affection, as each Grand Juror swears.

In 1842, Chicago was exceedingly depressed. Never perhaps more so. Our public credit was then exhausted, and labor on our public works had nearly or wholly ceased. The opinions I had expressed in 1837 were then repeated, and however strange it may appear, without offence. In 1842, when everyone desponded, I took occasion to remark as follows:

"Canal or no Canal, Chicago will advance. Her progress will be onward, and nothing, save some great calamity, can arrest her course, or the consumate folly, depravity, or imprudence of her people." Again, "You have been told that Chicago depends for her prosperity on the Canal. While I admit the Canal's importance, and look forward with the utmost confidence to its completion, I deny all such dependence. So long as yonder inland seas bear on their surface the wealth of every clime—so long as yonder fertile prairies bloom with verdure, and 'the cattle upon the thousand hills' shall graze their herbage, and so long as yonder interminable fields shall wave with their golden harvest, an effort to blot Chicago from existence, or to depress her rising consequence, would be like an attempt to quench the stars."

Having on that occasion prophesied a little, permit me, gentlemen, on this to prophesy a little more. There are persons now living (though not present) in Chicago who will see 5,000,000 of people in Illinois, and 200,000 in this

City,* a larger number than the Metropolis of England, in the reign of Queen Elizabeth, contained. This to some may problematically appear. It is, however, not only possible but probable, and I will tell you why. The State of Illinois contains 56,158 square miles of more fertile soil than any where exists. It is larger than New York, Ohio, or Pennsylvania. It contains more arable land than all New England, and more than England and Wales together. It is larger than Portugal and Denmark, and has more acres than Holland, Belgium, and Switzerland united. Twelve such States as Connecticut could be carved out of it and a fraction still be left. Were it as densely settled as Massachusetts is, it would contain that number now. Is it then, I ask, improbable that Illinois "in three score years and ten," will be as densely settled as Massachusetts is at present, and should the State contain 5,000,000, is 200,000 for Chicago an over-estimate?

In order, however, to insure her growth and her prosperity permanently secure, some effort will be necessary. Man is born to toil. Industry is essential to health and happiness, also to moral and intellectual improvement. Labor is a blessing only in disguise.

Among the means essential to our prosperity, good roads from here in all directions are pre-eminent. Not plank-roads existing on paper only, or on the pages of the revised Statutes of Illinois, like that from this City to Rockford,

---

* The writer was present when this Lecture was delivered at the "Old Court House," being one long, oblong apartment, capable of seating about 200 persons. And when the extravagant prediction was made *"that persons were now living (though not present) in Chicago who will see 200.000 people in this City!"* An *uproarious laugh of incredulity* convulsed the entire audience. And yet, the Orator so far doubted his own statement that he could not venture to say, that the persons *then living, who would see this City contain 200,000 people*, were in Chicago or in his hearing.

But time, has not only verified his statement, that the *persons were then living who should see this;* but further, and far beyond his exceedingly, what seemed extravagant prediction, there were *then listening to his own lecture*, in that room, at least *twenty* or *thirty persons*, who, *living in Chicago* then, have lived to see it contain over 400,000, or double the number of people estimated, and that too, before the lapse of 30 years.

about which much has been said and little done. Nor
railroads, such as were made a few nights since, at a
meeting here, which it is feared will sleep the sleep of
death; but plank-roads, railroads, and good common roads,
upon the earth's broad surface, which common people
delight to travel.

It is, therefore, gentlemen, to be regretted deeply, so I
think, that our Legislature at its last session should have
repealed the law, requiring labor during the last year to be
performed on public roads, as also the law, authorizing the
imposition of a small tax for their improvement.   This fact
is not generally known.   It is nevertheless so.

In 1841, a law was passed, authorizing the County Com-
missioners' Court, to require from one to five day's labor
from each able-bodied man, between 21 and 50, in Illinois,
to be laid out on the public highways.

In 1843, a law was passed imposing a small tax for their
improvement.

On the 28th of February, 1845, these laws were both
unfortunately repealed.   Another was substituted in their
stead, but so imperfect in its provisions, that it became
entirely useless.   It gave no authority to collect a tax or
penalty.

The general road act, passed March 3, 1845, made no
provision for that year.   Of course, the State of Illinois,.
during the whole of 1845, was without a road act.

Fortunately, however, it was of but little inconvenience.
The laws of Illinois, like *some* of the fixed stars whose light,
it is said, has not yet reached us, and like others, although
extinguished some time since, continued yet to shine on, so
exceedingly tardy in their progress that their passage and
their repeal is not essential in every instance till months, and
sometimes years, we are told, thereafter.   Besides, the people of this State are "a law-abiding people."   The repeal,
then, of a salutary statute, had it been known, would not
have prevented labor from being so essential to our prosperity.

When the Parthenon, or temple of Minerva, at Athens,
was completed, the oxen, which for years had been accustomed to draw stone from the quarry to the Acropolis, were
discharged from further service, and, as a mark of special
favor, thenceforth permitted to graze on the public com-
mons.   Sometime thereafter a celebration took place in the·

city, and a procession was formed from thence or the lower town to the Acropolis.—In that procession, a large number of oxen in their yokes were introduced, to fill the pageant. The oxen before discharged perceiving others about to perform a task which had (as they supposed) for years devolved on them, took their position without drivers in the line, and performed the route as regularly as before. It is just so with the people of Illinois. Accustomed to "mend their ways," without a legal requisition for that purpose, they have hitherto, and it is hoped will continue thus to do, "law or no law."

A writer (an enthusiast of course), some years ago, in speaking of rivers and their use, observed, they were designed to feed canals—and Talleyrand, Napoleon's prime minister, for many years, is represented, though perhaps untruly, to have said that "language was invented to conceal our thoughts." Northern Illinois, by our Creator, was designed for no fictitious purpose. It is adapted in a peculiar manner for either railroads, plank-roads, common roads, or canals; and nothing but an effort in behalf of her people is required to complete them altogether. Of the Canal it is useless now to speak. A promise, a mere promise by our Legislature, (accompanied by a grant which renders its violation impossible) to withhold their sacrilegious hands from its remaining funds, has not only its completion perfectly secured, but the payment in half a century or so of all the debt hitherto incurred for its construction, and, in part, the redemption of our country's honor. Two years will witness its completion, and the wealth of other realms in triumph floating on its surface.

The question having frequently been asked, whether the completion of the Illinois and Michigan Canal will benefit Chicago or no. Allow me, gentlemen, here to say, it will, in a thousand different ways. Time will not permit me now to illustrate this position. I hope, however, the question will, sometime during the season, be debated here, and then each one will have an opportunity to be heard.

There is another subject, gentlemen, which, at the present time, bears heavily upon us. I now allude to a railroad from Chicago to the Mississippi. It is not my intention here to speak of Whitney's road, because his views upon the subject are, I think, erroneous, and his plans wholly impracticable. A railroad, however, from the Atlantic cities to the Mississippi, and westward thence,* is just as sure of its completion in our day and generation as the sparks are to fly upward. That road must, of course, pass around the southern extremity of Lake Michigan; and, unless we are wise, it may perhaps go further south, and escape Chicago altogether. If a railroad from here to Galena, or to the Mississippi, was now completed, or in progress, is it not more than probable that such road would be a connecting link between the East and the " Far West?" The progress of empire, since the morning stars first sang together, has been westward. The Euphrates' banks received from the Almighty Earth's first tenants. Greece shortly to power and fame succeeded. Rome afterwards supplanted Greece in her career, and Western Europe, on her ruins, thereafter rose to empire—

> "Rome heard the Gothic trumpets' blast,
> The march of hosts as Alaric past."

England, the land of scholars and the men of arms, is rotten ere she is ripe—

> "A Queen upon a throne of Gold,
> A Parliament of drones;
> A Nation's voice that's bought and sold,
> While every cottage groans."

Our country, gentlemen, is destined shortly to become

---

* It is a singular verification of this Orator's statements, that in this very year 1846, the Whitney project, for a GREAT PACIFIC RAIL-ROAD from the Mississippi, was proposed to Congress by a MEMORIAL. This was referred to the Committee on Public Lands, of which Judge Breese, of the Supreme Court of this State, was then Chairman.   That HE made a Report thereon, which was published.   This Report favors the construction of the Road, though not on the WHITNEY project. The Report is remarkable for the accuracy of detail—knowledge—it manifests, in tracing out the lines upon which it has been built through the great South Pass of the Mountains; and in suggesting the practical means which were adopted long afterwards, in 1863; when the gigantic nature of the undertaking seemed *feasible* to Congress: Though, at the time, the Report was made, all its facts and details, as well as the enterprise itself, were treated with derision and ridicule, by as great an authority in the U. S. Senate of those days as the late "Thomas H. Benton, of Missouri."   And yet, while Breese wears no garland, is honored by no *memorial*—a *statue*, in marble, of *Benton* as author of the Road to the Pacific—honors his memory in the St. Louis Merchants' Exchange.

the seat of wealth, the source of power, the home of learn-
ing, and we hope the abode of virtue. And Chicago is
destined also to much honor. Her position is commanding
and her progress sure. I saw, in an English paper, a short
time since, New York, Chicago, and New Orleans put down
as three of the most prominent points in our Republic.—
The Rev. Sidney Smith, now deceased, prebend of St.
Paul's, the projector, with Lord Brougham and others, of
the *Edinburgh Review*, better known in this country for his
remarks in relation to some Pennsylvania bonds, of which
he had unfortunately became the owner, in a letter dated
at London, on the 28th of August, 1845, directed to a gentleman in this city, says: "The spot from which I write
(London) was considered by the Romans as the end of the
world—the spot from which you write (Chicago), remote as
it seems, may become hereafter the centre of civilization."
And why, I would ask, gentlemen, may it not be so? It is
but a short time since, and within the recollection of many
of us now present, when the population of those States was
mostly on the other side of the Alleganies. Where is it
now? A majority of the whole is west thereof, and that
majority rapidly increasing. In order, however, that we
may fulfil the destiny that awaits us here, much is to be
done. Industry and economy are not only the parents of
every virtue, but the cause of a nation's, as well as of an
individual's, prosperity.

The City of Chicago, since her incorporation, the County
of Cook, since known as such, and the State of Illinois,
since her admission into the Union, have erred exceedingly
in their financial operations. I hazard nothing, I believe,
in saying, that one-half of the moneys raised by taxation,
by each, and borrowed, for which we are now indebted, had
it been juduciously expended, would have effected more
than the whole has done under our present system. Of
this, gentleman, I speak with confidence—and in some
cases with knowledge too. In others, I speak from facts,
which cannot err.

The exposition of fraud and error—of wrong and outrage,
and the suggestion of improvements to correct those errors,
and remedy those wrongs and outrages, is at times an un-
gracious task, and not unfrequently with danger is attended.

When the great Earl of Chatham, "'mid England's peers,
arose and said he would not sit quiet when his liberty was

invaded, nor look in silence on public robbery," it was
thought by many a bold speech—and the event the asser-
tion justified. Relying upon his own resources, the petty
knaves, the acknowledged fools, and the conceded villains
throughout the realm, were from his counsels totally excluded. They, of course, combined against him, and, by
the aid of England's aristocracy, more corrupt if possible
still, ousted the patriot and statesman from place and
power. Posterity, however, reversed afterward their judg-
ment, and did him full and ample justice.

> "The eagle flies alone, the geese in flocks:
> Sheep herd together, and wolves and jackals
> In packs their prey pursue."

Time would fail me were I on this occasion to investigate
the origin, and trace the progress of our enormous debt,*

* We have looked up the records for this *"enormous* debt," of which
the eloquent orator is speaking, and find that the *debt* of Chicago was

In 1838,			$9,996.54	In 1842,			$16,337.01
" 1839,			7,182.25	" 1843,			12,655.40
" 1840,			6,559.63	" 1846, not over			15,000.00
" 1841,			12,387.67				

The State debt of that time, to which he refers in the text, was
about $20,000,000; two millions of this had been borrowed abroad to
complete the Illinois and Michigan Canal. The State failed to pay
her interest on the debt in 1838–9. and the work on the Canal ceased;
contractors failed; and the construction was for the time abandoned, it
was not again resumed until the year 1845. In March of that year, an
Act was passed, providing that if the holders of Canal bonds would
advance a sum sufficient to complete the Canal, the State would con-
vey to trustees, for their security and the repayment of all moneys
advanced by them, all the Canal lands remaining unsold, which Congress had donated to aid the State, in the completion of the improvement: the Canal itself, so far as it had been constructed—and, *all tolls
to be received after its completion,* until the whole amount of all moneys
borrowed, known as the Canal debt, with interest, should be paid to
the holders of Canal bonds.

Under this Act, the property was conveyed to Trustees—*two* on the
part of the bond-holders, and *one* State Trustee, by whom the Canal
lands were sold. The Canal was finished in 1847, and opened to *business* in *1848;* and the whole debt has been paid from the moneys
received from sales of land and tolls, and the Canal has become a
source of revenue to the State as well as its property. As regards the

which, like an incubus, hangs heavily upon us, or show how and for what purpose a million and a half or more of our bonds are now, like Milton's angels, floating upon the vast abyss, without a parent, a patron, or a friend, for which the State has yet received no compensation, and for which none, I believe, is expected. Our whole financial system seems to me, gentlemen, like

> "The application
> Of homœopathic medicines to
> Arrest the earthquake and to quench volcanoes."

The time, however, it is hoped, will come when some one will be to Illinois her guardian angel—who, as a distinguished senator and statesman (Col. Young, of New York) observes, "will confound and paralyze the congregated energies of corruption, and rescue from the lowest depths of degradation the lost credit of the State; who will, from under the huge mass of documentary rubbish, disinter the enormous skull, the disjointed vertebræ, and scattered bones of the mammoth debt that has been accumulated by millions, and bonds therefor poured out (sometimes without consideration) like water, till the drunkenness of financial debauchery has eventuated in *delirium tremens*— some one who will collate, describe, systematize, and arrange the repulsive fragments of this fiscal anatomy, so that its frightful skeleton may be seen at one view, and held up in all its enormities to the public gaze, as a memento of the past and a warning to the future."

I have heard it frequently stated, and in Chicago too, by men of wealth and standing, from whom much better things are, or ought to have been, expected, that we must not scrutinize these things too closely, for peradventure friends may suffer. Gracious and eternal God! why are thy bolts withheld when doctrines such as these, without excuse and without apology, escape from polluted lips?—Such doctrines, however, (thanks to heaven!) meet with countenance from none but knaves. They are not the principles of *pure* democracy, and I hope not of whiggery. Let no such man be trusted. He is an enemy to his country, and a traitor to his trust—a nuisance to his party and an outlaw from his God. No honor, surely, can await him here. Let him

City, in the years 1840 and 1841, Mr. Thomas Hoyne, who was then the *City Clerk*, says: that *he kept* and *revised all the Tax rolls of these two years*; and the *whole amount, real estate tax or revenue, in 1841, was $7000!!* about $8000 or $9000 in 1842.

then go to where he belongs, where his talents will be duly
appreciated, and feed for hire the half-starved swine that
prowl about hell's dormitory, or the backdoor of mammon's
cellar kitchen.

"Six thousand years of sorrow have well nigh
Fulfilled their tardy and disastrous course,"

Since the Almighty, by a deed of trust, gave Adam and his
posterity the globe we inherit, and the appurtenances there-
unto belonging— including every herb, and every tree—save
one, and every fowl, and every fish, and every beast, and
every living thing that moveth on the earth.   For what
purpose?   That he might replenish it, and subdue it—that
he might, as in the case of Eden, "dress it and keep it."
How, gentlemen, I ask, have we discharged that trust?   An
answer to this inquiry can hardly be expected in one discourse.   Our business, therefore, is at present with that
portion of Adam's posterity which has taken up its resi-
dence in Chicago and its vicinity.

The red man of the woods, who preceded us in possession here, violated, it seems, his trust, or rather neglected
it, and when the bugle notes of civilization sounded in his
ears, he fled far away.   After a possession (as presumed)
of several centuries, he left nothing but the names of lakes
and rivers—of mountains and of plains, to mark the spot
o'er which he wandered.   I think, therefore, of savage man
but little—and of the white man, who is a savage, less.   It
is mind alone that "makes the man, the want of it the"—
animal.

That portion of Adam's posterity residing here is now
composed of matter various and discordant.   A writer, of
some eminence, once, as we are told, divided mankind into
two general divisions—those who are *in* the penitentiary
and those who are *out*.   This division is too unequal for
any use.   Were perfect justice done on earth, they might
perhaps be more equal.   But, as it is, other divisions must
be adopted.   I have, therefore, thought of another equally
absurd, and, as some pretend, equally unequal—those who
are *are*, and those who *are not*, their own worst enemies.

The last, to-wit: those who are *not* their own worst enemies, I need not speak of.   Of them, Christianity has care
—a name how glorious—its founder in rags—a mountain,
as Whitfield said, for his pulpit, and the whole arch of heaven for his sounding-board.   Its apostles uneducated fisher-

men—with poverty for its throne—a staff for its sceptre—a crown of thorns for its diadem, it went forth conquering and to conquer.   Thrones and dominions, principalities and powers fell before it, and Paganism, at its approach, dissolved as "flax at the touch of fire."   It reached at length Chicago, and sixteen, or seventeen, or eighteen churches mark its triumph.

> "Who is this that comes from Eden?
> 'Tis the Saviour, now victorious,
> Traveling westward in his might;
> 'Tis the Saviour, O how glorious
> To his people in their sight.
> Satan conquered, and the grave,
> Jesus now is strong to save."

Those who are their own worst enemies are like the polypus:—divide it and it becomes two polipi—divide it again, and yet again, the same result succeeds.   Hence the division of mankind into moral, political, and religious parties. Religious parties—that is, pure religious parties, it is true, are anomalies.   We mean by them such only as are religious by profession merely—those, as Pollock says:

> "Who put a sixpence in the urn
> Of charity, and take a shilling out
> To keep it sounding."

To treat of each would far exceed the time and space allotted me.   I therefore must be brief.

Public opinion, we are told, is not like the maiden wooed, but like the widow won.   It is also like the nettle—touch it lightly and the finger bleeds; grasp it firmly with a giant's grasp, and it to the pressure yields, and in the hand "harmless as dreams of babes become."   The politician's temple stands, we are informed, upon base built on sand, in the centre of a wide extended prairie, accessible only to eagles and to reptiles.   While the former attain its summit by the boldness of their flight, the latter reach the same object by tortuous paths, themselves with slime all covered over, and they in their turn covering those who aid them to ascend.

> "Unblest by virtue, government a league
> Becomes—a circling junto of the great,
> To rob by law."

But, gentlemen, of this enough.   I may hereafter resume the subject.   The field is ample, and the laborers few.   Its portals, however, are so guarded that no one has dared, as yet, to enter it.   It is time for some one to begin.   A victory would be certain.

When Suwarrow commanded a Russian army of some 20,000, upon the Turkish border, he was told that an overwhelming force was gathering to attack him. Without waiting for its concentration, he issued an order, as follows:

"I understand there are but 50,000 Turks opposed to us, and 50,000 more within a day's march. It were better were they all here, so that they might all be beaten on the same day, but as it is otherwise, we may as well begin with these."

An attack was made next morning, and the 50,000 Turks cut to pieces; the other 50,000 arrived in the evening, and were cut to pieces also.

Northern Illinois has never been so prosperous as now. Industry never so abundant; and economy (except adversity compelling) so prevalent before. This prosperity, however, is owing not to speculation, nor legislation, but to the might, as Cowper says, "that slumbers in the peasant's arms." The efforts, the united efforts of a whole people judiciously directed.

I may, and probably shall be, charged "with using up all the big I's in this discourse, and leaving, therefore, none for you." The allusion some may, and some may not, understand. Permit me then to explain:

Some years ago, Governor Reynolds, of Illinois, usually called "the Old Ranger," became a candidate for governor in this State. Gov. Edwards, who had been elected sometime before, became also a candidate, at the same time, for re-election. Reynolds, it is said, was illiterate; Edwards, "a gentleman and a scholar." The former, in a letter, speaking of himself, used, we are told, a small i instead of of a large I. This being public, became a subject of no little merriment to his opponent, and was, unfortunately, alluded to in a stump speech, by Gov. Edwards. The old Ranger, however, in his reply, observed that his opponent had used up all the big I's, and left none for him; he had therefore used the small i from pure necessity. It needs no prophet's ken to tell who gained the palm.

It is not, however, true that all the big I's are yet absorbed. Enough, I apprehend, remain for all. You will, therefore, I hope and trust, come forward this evening, and take the "Sheridan Oath."

This allusion may to some be as inexplicable as that already made to the "Old Ranger." Allow me, then, to explain this also. Richard Brinsley Sheridan, who afterwards became one of the most finished orators in Britain, in some of his first attempts was unsuccessful. On "breaking down" the third or fourth time, and being rallied by his boon companions, he tartly replied: "I know it is in me, and, by God, it shall come out."

Few know their capacity for public speaking, until the attempt is made and frequently repeated. The opportunity here presented is a good one. The whole world (for subjects) is before us, our room convenient, our audience respectable, and those who neglect it must, of course, be exceedingly reprehensible.

A few words, gentlemen, on the philosophy of human life, and I will close.

Charles James Fox, the celebrated English orator and statesman, in speaking of this world, observes:

"'Tis a very good world that we live in,
To lend, to spend, or to give in;
But to beg, to borrow, or get a man's own,
'Tis the very worst world that ever was known."

I do not, gentlemen, subscribe to all this. The above must, I think, have been written by Fox in his desponding moments. My sentiments upon this subject are better expressed in the following lines, which have just been handed me to read on this occasion; to the views therein expressed, I subscribe and recommend them to you for deliberate consideration. They are entitled "The World as it Is."

This world is not so bad a world
  As some would like to make it:
Though whether good, or whether bad,
  Depends on how we take it.
For if we scold and fret all day,
  From dewey morn till even,
This world will ne'er afford to man
  A foretaste here of heaven.

This world in truth's as good a world
  As e'er was known to any,
Who have not seen another yet,
  And these are very many.
And if the men, and women too,
  Have plenty of employment,
Those surely must be hard to please
  Who cannot find enjoyment.

This word is quite a pleasant world,
  In rain or pleasant weather,
If people would but learn to live
  In harmony together:
Nor cease to burst the kindling bond
  By love and peace cemented,
And learn that best of lessons yet,
  To always be contented.

Then were the world a pleasant world,
  And pleasant folks were in it.
The day would pass most pleasantly,
  To those who thus began it.
To all the nameless grievances,
  Brought on by borrowed troubles,
Would prove, as certainly they are,
  A mass of empty bubbles!

Dr. Paley, a celebrated divine, the author of "Moral Philosophy," "Natural Theology," and several other works of the highest reputation, used to say, that "A man must play the fool about one-half of his time in order to avoid being a fool for the residue."

The celebrated Robert Hall, whose sermons many of you

have doubtless read and, if so, admired, being once repri-
manded by a dignified though simple clergyman, for his
levity of manner out of the pulpit, replied, "There, brother,
you and I differ; you talk nonsense in the pulpit and I out
of it."

"Gravity," says a distinguished French author, "is a
mysterious invention or contrivance of the body to conceal
defects in the brain."

It is hardly worth our while then to affect gravity or dignity in cases where it is not required, and where an attempt
to do so would make us only ridiculous.   On proper occa-
sions, I have no doubt both will be regarded by every
member of this Lyceum, not only here but elsewhere, and
"dignity of soul" always.

I thank you, ladies and gentlemen, for the patience you
have manifested on this occasion, and promise never more
to offend in like manner, so long.

I have now, as Cowper observes,

> " Roved for fruit,
> Roved far and gathered much: Some harsh 'tis true,
> Plucked from the thorns and briars of reproof,
> But wholesome, well digested."

And can I think with Scott, surely say, that

> "To his promise just,
> Vich-Alpine hath discharged his trust.
> Hath led thee safe, through watch and ward,
> Far past Clan-Alpine's outmost guard."

I propose now, gentlemen, to leave you at Coilantogle
ford.

> "And thou must keep thee with thy sword."

Let me say to you, on this occasion, as Campbell does
on another:

> " Wave Munich, all your banners wave,
> And charge with all your chivalry."

And should you in the contest fall, remember with old
Homer:

> " Such honors Ilion to her hero paid,
> And peaceful slept the mighty Hector's shade."

But, gentlemen, with proper efforts you will not fail. It
is impossible, wholly impossible.   Allow me then to close
in one of Scott's beautiful strains, which describes your
situation, condition, and duty, as well as mine:

> " 'Charge, Chester, charge! On, Stanley, on!'
> Were the last words of Marmion."

RISE AND PROGRESS OF CHICAGO.

The moon shines dimly just after the sun has set. To give reminiscences of the early history of Chicago in a form that would be likely to interest you, particularly after having listened to the lofty aspirations and eloquent discoursings of a Wentworth, Bross, Balestier, and others who have favored us upon this subject with gems from the well-filled storehouse of their polished and cultivated intellects, is a task that I might well shrink from, and be a silent admirer of the rich developments of these faithful biographers, rather than attempt any elaborate description of its early progress myself; but, however much may have been said, there is still room for the further unfolding of its primitive doings and wonderful strides to popularity and greatness.

It is not our purpose to trace the present popularity and important advancement of Chicago, from the early explorers of the great North-west, down through past ages, to the probable discovery of a point on Lake Michigan, that was destined to be, in the distant future, the Metropolis of the Universe, that, to our mind, would be too chimerical, and fraught with too much uncertainty to command respectful consideration; but, as near as memory will permit, to "hold the mirror up to nature," and relate some of the more prominent features of its progress within the memory of its "oldest inhabitants" now resident among us, many of whom deserve honorable mention; we might also name those who have done much toward enhancing the growth, importance, and prosperity of Chicago; but where all have done so well it would be invidious to particularize, we will, therefore, content ourself by at once giving our personal experience of the early rise and growth of the City of the West.

Let us, for a moment, remove the veil, and take a retrospect of the past forty-five years, we will then have disclosed to view a barren waste, the abode of the timid fawn, the deer, the wolf, and tawny Indian, whose bark alone skimmed along these majestic lakes, claiming the ownership of their pure and limpid waters. Now mark the change! These lofty spires that rise to their graceful and giddy heights; the busy mill and spacious warehouse; the stately mansion and lowly cot, around whose slender portals the woodbine entwines its caressing tendrils. We might extend the view, and admire the dottings of civilization and culture in the innumerable cottages and pretentious farm-houses that nestle among the tall grass and fringe the borders of our rivers and woodlands, but our purpose just now is a review of the early history and doings of Chicago.

When we first landed on these shores, our impression was that it might be a place of some importance, were it not so low, and I ventured to record my hastily-conceived views upon the register of the hotel where we remained for a few hours: my entry ran something like this: "April 20, 1832. James A. Marshall, Ogdensburgh, New York; this might be a place of some importance, but the ground is too low." Two or three hours afterward, I chanced to look over the quire of paper dubbed a register, and found added to my remarks, "Solomon 2d." I *looked* wise for a moment, but *felt* that my talent had been over-estimated, and have never since undertaken to be wiser than my friend, whom, I afterward learned, honored me with that illustrious appellation. I found the place too small for me to hope to make anything by my profession (a physician), the garrison being supplied with one of the best in the country in the person of Dr. Philip Maxwell, so we shipped at once for Navarino, Green Bay, Wis., where we landed in time to see three soldiers branded and drummed out of camp, also to see the payment of 7000 Indians by Col. Boyd. I remained at Navarino until August 5th, 1834, when I sailed in the Schooner Nancy Dousman, Capt. Saunders, for Chicago. After a very boisterous passage, we arrived on the 15th of the same month, where I have resided, with the exception of one year only, ever since.

To undertake the recital of all, or even many of the

prominent causes of Chicago's rise and wonderful progress
within the past forty-five years, and do justice to the subject, would occupy more time than could be devoted to
one lecture, unless it were prolonged to an unreasonable
length, and thereby losing much of its intended usefulness;
we will, therefore, to relieve our subject from the dull
monotony incident to the recital of statistical forms, for
the time being, fancy ourselves in an artist's studio, invit-
ing him, with canvas, paint, and brush, to create his ideal
of a great and marvelous city, of less than half a century's
growth, drawing from the resources of his imaginative
genius all that could give it *eclat* and beauty, his subject
a low, uninviting marsh, a sluggish stream on one side, a
bold, majestic lake in front, an extended prairie behind;
with this unseemly background we will watch his progress
in filling out the picture. On the right, as you face the
north, is a group of one-story block houses, surrounded
by a high fence; the two-story buildings at the east of the
hollow square are the quarters of the commandant and
officers; that hip-roofed, square block-house, with a row of
small port-holes, is the look-out, where sentinels are placed
to watch the approach of hostile Indians, the lower part
used as a guard-house—that is Fort Dearborn; the river
meandering its way around the east side of the fort, running southward, mingling with the lake at Madison street,
east of which is a peninsula connecting the north and
south sides of the river (and was the only point, forty-three
years ago, of ingress and egress for vessels to and from
Lake Michigan, until March, 1833, when the spring freshet,
accompanied by a violent storm, forced a direct channel
to the lake, which was afterward dredged and piers run
out, by direction of the Government, and which now forms
the fine harbor for the white-winged messengers that enrich
our country by their precious burdens). We will accom-
pany our artist a little farther; at the left of the fort, and
running west, are a few modest structures, designed, apparently, for the double purpose of stores and dwellings, ex-
tending west as far as Dearborn street (there the business
portion of the village, for a time, rested; south of Lake
and east of Dearborn streets, for three or four blocks, was
a corn and potato field. The principal forwarding business
was done on the north side of the Chicago River for several

years, but the personal interest and enterprise of a few gentlemen residing on the South Side, who had considerable
real estate unoccupied, changed the channel of business by
building warehouses on that side of the river, after which it
was transacted there; indeed, the North Side never recovered
its former business prestige, but contented itself by building palatial residences, and being considered the place *par
excellence*, and the home of the *élite* of Chicago). We next
observe a ferry crossing the river at Dearborn street, con-
nected by a rope attached to a windlass at each side of
the river, and a scow in the centre, propelled by hand
power, placed there for the convenience of the residents
of both sides of the river. This rude piece of mechanism
remained there until a Mr. Norton erected a draw-bridge,
spanning the river at the same place where the old scow
had done such good service for so long a time, but whose
occupation, like Othello's, was now gone. It was igno-
miniously torn from its moorings to make room for the
unwieldy structure that supplanted it. From this time
onward the city grew rapidly, and from this time may be
dated the commencement of its now universal popularity.
We will now leave our artist to finish the picture as it
may best suit his own ideality. Some new beauty is now
developed — some wonderful advancement made in the
growth and importance of the painted city; the unfinished
streets show marks of improvement, lined with palatial
business structures, ponderous warehouses, elegant and
elaborate places of worship, halls of justice clothed in
Oriental magnificence, school-houses with substantial ex-
teriors are brought to view, avenues laid out and lined
with costly marble mansions, parks and boulevards gem
the environs with rare exotics and elaborately ornamental,
varied, and beautiful foliage, the streets are as smooth as
parlor floors; nothing is left undone that imaginative genius
could invent to make a city that would be the wonder
and admiration of the civilized world. The picture completed is heralded beyond the seas, sent broadcast among
the cities of the east, and presented to the wealthy, the
intellectual, and the enterprising of our own land; they
shrug their shoulders knowingly, acknowledging its great
beauty and the consummate ideality of the artist, but
think that he has devoted too much to the imaginative

to assume a reality among the cities of the world, turning from what they supposed the visionary imaginings of a fertile brain and elaborate brush to something more substantial and real. The artist invites their presence to witness the last finishing touch, then with unbounded confidence in himself, he traces the name CHICAGO. The multitude exclaims, " It is no ideal, but a veritable reality, and now stands the wonder of the universe."

Thus we have presented, in a feeble way, but a bird's-eye view of the germ of our present great Metropolis; its early outlook by no means calculated to encourage the enterprising explorer, has been brought to view: and watching with marked interest the unparalleled improvement on every hand, we are awed into silence, and dare not prophesy its future greatness. As the sturdy farmer scans his field but lately cleared of a cumbrous undergrowth of shrubs and thickets, the ground untilled, the seed unsown—glowing prospects of a rich harvest are least suggesting, but, when with implements of agriculture and determined will, he delves and toils from morn till night, faith spurs him on, and slowly, but surely, the planted seed, the budding stalk, and waving grain, insure a harvest, and recompense is nigh. So to the early settler, Chicago stood desolate and alone, the undergrowth of uncivilized Indian habitation lent an uninviting aspect to the eastern world, and advancement, for the time being, seemed impossible; but the rich soil of natural advantages was unearthed by the foresight of our pioneers, the seed planted, then arose in plenteous harvest, the wonderful products of a new-made vineyard, until now, after a growth of forty years, the City sketched upon the canvas, loses its primitive indentity, and stands before the world a marvel.

This picture, however, portrays but the outward part of Chicago's greatness, it is the internal workings that have given it the wonderful celebrity that it now enjoys. Let us, for a moment, glance at some of these causes which have led to and done so much toward its advancement. First, its location, being at the head of lake navigation and the only prominent lake frontage that the State of Illinois has for the receipt and transportation of her vast agricultural and mineral resources, thereby enjoying some State pride. Again, the immense lumber interests form a large share of

consideration; from a beginning. within the time indicated
at the commencement of these remarks, of 100,000,000
feet. it has now increased to more than 1,500,000,000 feet
per annum.   The cereal products, too, which here find a
market and outlet, have increased from 5000 bushels in
the year 1834 to more than 15,000,000 bushels per annum;
nor is this all, the pork product advancing from 500 to
over 1,500,000 hogs packed every year, aside from those
used for home consumption.   In our monetary exchange,
how wonderful the advance, from $25,000 per week, which
at that time indicated marked progress, it now requires
more than $20,000,000 to do a week's financial business.
The advancement in general business, too, is well calculated to amaze the mere casual observer, from an insignificant sum of a few thousand dollars required to transact
our annual business forty-three years ago, the enormous
sum of more than $200,000,000 is now necessary to sat-
isfy the demands of the thousands who look to Chicago
for their supplies.   Out of the fifteen billions of dollars annually required to feed and clothe the people of the United
States, one hundred and twenty-five millions of that sum is
necessary to feed and clothe the citizens of Chicago for the
same time.

We might go on, *ad libitum*, enumerating the capacious
and unparalleled increase in the innumerable branches of
industry that are adding so much to the importance, and
expanding the area of our city to its present ponderous
proportions; but enough has already been noticed to sat-
isfy, without doubt, the most sceptical of its admirers.
But perhaps the most wonderful rise in values has taken
place in real estate; property that, in 1834, sold for $200
per lot of 50 feet, has been sold within the past year
for $2000 per foot, being an advance of $99,800 from
the original purchase; this, however, cannot be considered
a fair criterion of the general advancement of real estate,
nevertheless, the increase has been, upon an average,
since the time specified, about four hundred per cent.
of its original value; still, it fluctuated more or less until
the commencement of the Canal land sales in 1848, since
then, real estate has been reckoned according to prices
at which it sold at that time. and for a number of years
afterward, sales were negotiated upon Canal time, or

Canal terms, as it was called—that was, one-fourth cash, balance in one, two, and three years, with interest at six per cent. per annum, payable annually in advance. The wealth of some of our millionaires may, therefore, be dated from that time, as few could boast of more than their thousands until the Canal sales, which placed an estimated value upon real estate, furnishing a new impetus to all branches of business. To the Canal sales, then, of 1848 to 1853, when more than $3,000,000 worth of property was sold (all of which I sold at public sale), is due the credit of advancing the pecuniary interests of our fellow-citizens more than any other circumstance since the foundation of the city government. Taking advantage of the low prices at which Canal property sold, they purchased, and having the sagacity, some of them, to hold on to their purchases, they increased in value upon their hands, and made them rich. The peculiar location, superior agricultural and internal advantages, railroad facilities, water communication, and enterprise of our citizens combined, is what has given to Chicago its eminence at home and abroad, and *not*, as some have supposed, the sagacity and enterprise of a few of the more fortunate of our fellow-citizens, who, for want of purchasers at the time that they desired to sell, were obliged to hold on to their property, thereby becoming wealthy, more by reason of their misfortune—or rather, their good fortune—in being unable to sell. Nevertheless, great credit is due them for their liberality in using their wealth in the erection of elegant structures, and in otherwise lending their aid in beautifying and adorning our city.

Many, however, who took a prominent part in the building up and advancing the growth and prosperity of our City, have passed away, leaving names not recorded in the activities of life, but graven indelibly upon the memories of their fellow-citizens, and are justly extolled for their upright lives and many virtues. Those of the pioneers who remain to witness the further growth of their favorite and patron city speak gently of the departed, but, with pride in their name and tireless enterprise, point to the vast resources of our wonderful City, and say, "these are their eulogies, it needs no marble column to tell of their greatness, their

deeds are written in the early annals of famed Chicago."
Many of them did not live to witness its sudden destruc-
tion and succeeding rapid progress. But, in the dawning
years of our City's eminence, was established—the energy,
strength, and ground work of the enterprise that bid it
rise.

The great and unprecedented increase of our population
may be, and, perhaps, is, attributable to the widespread in-
formation given of its superior advantages, particularly so
since the fire of 1871.

A catastrophy that will never be obliterated from the
memory of those who witnessed the awful spectacle, a scene
of grandeur and sublimity unparalleled in the history of the
world's conflagrations,—the accumulated wealth of many
years swept away in an hour; the millionnaire of yesterday,
to-day walks hand in hand with poverty; the prospects of
a competence in after years silenced forever. Thus we
contemplated when viewing the fire of Oct. 9, 1871. After
the great holocaust had given way to smouldering *débris*,
with others, we strolled among the ruins, meeting at almost
every step some well-known friend, whose life's earnings
had been sacrificed through the carelessness of irresponsi-
ble parties. One friend in particular, who had been one
of the most unfortunate of the wealthy men of our City,
I thus accosted, after offering my sympathy: "Mr. C***,
you must be one of the heaviest losers by the fire;" he
smiled pleasantly, and answerd, "I have lost heavily, it
is true, but I am not discouraged; in ten years, Chicago will be a greater City than it ever was, and I shall do
my share to make it so;" and he has kept his word. From
that time onward, the City was the centre of interest and
attraction. Many who came were deeply interested in what
they saw, and were conquered by the veritable facts visible
before them, and not only remained themselves, but advised
their friends to come to this eldorado of the west; the result,
as shown, is, that since the time stated, our population
has increased a thousand-fold, from 500 inhabitants forty-
three years ago, we have now more than 500,000, according to estimates recently made, and still they come. Our
public school-houses—or rather, our school-house—then
contained less than 100 pupils; now, more than 40,000

children congregate and occupy seats provided for them in our commodious and imposingly-built public school edifices, fitting these thousands of immortal minds for usefulness and honor, preparing them to take part in the great panorama of life. Aside from this formidable array of young ideas that sip knowledge from the public fountain, there are a number of private institutions, colleges, and seminaries, occupied by some thousands of the children whose parents prefer this manner of instruction. Thus, it will be seen, that while we have been engaged, and seemingly bound to the all-absorbing influence of gain, the rising generation has not been forgotten, means have been provided for the ample development of their mental faculties, intellectual aspirations, and moral culture. All honor is due to our sagacious law makers for these timely safeguards. May free schools, free speech, and a free press continue to be the law of the land, although the latter has often been abused by the injudicious management of unthinking and unprincipled men, nevertheless, it had better be so than to interfere with its freedom.

A due and proper regard for moral and religious rights is incumbent upon all good citizens; the free discussion of their favorite dogmas is allowable throughout the length and breadth of our land, and there let it remain—further recognition is dangerous to the peace and well-being of our country, as well as to our individual privileges.

It is not to be supposed that these many years of prosperity and wonderful advancement have been allowed to pass without some intervening incidents, which, at the time, were fraught with more or less amusement and enjoyment. Although time has transformed the ambitious and ever-restless youth into matured manhood, and some into declining life, yet, in calling the roll of time *backward*, we find recorded many laughable and ludicrous incidents. We will omit several amusing anecdotes for want of time to relate them; there are a few, however, which I think that I shall always remember. Many of our older settlers will recollect the old Presbyterian Church, located near the S.-W. corner of Clark and Lake streets. We were in the habit then, as now, of holding Wednesday evening prayer-meetings; that most excellent man, Rev. Jeremiah Porter, had left us, in his place was a dashing, eloquent young preacher,

bran-new from college, but entirely unfitted to occupy th
position he was called to fill. After these meetings th
pastor would hasten from the speaker's desk and offer hi
services. as a general thing, to one of the prettiest youn
ladies present. Of course, he was rarely, if ever, refusec
Upon the particular evening in question, he approached
young lady of exceeding beauty, proffering his services a
chaperon, which were accepted. At the same time, I ha
the honor of escorting a near relative of the lady allude
to, and for whose domicile we were all bound, the part
of the first part taking the lead; the night was extremel
dark, and, not having the advantage of street lamps an
gas-light, we had to *feel* our way along; it was just afte
a very profuse rain, our streets — without sidewalks e
any such thing, — were very unpleasant thoroughfares.-
We had not proceeded far, when we heard a shriek fro
the young lady, and an "Oh, dear me! Where are w
going?" from the reverend gentleman. Another shrie
then one more, still louder, *en concert*, proceeded from o
the more than Egyptian-darkness, when the lady at my sic
exclaimed, in alarm, "Mr. Marshall, what is the matter:
"Oh, nothing more," I replied, "than that Mr. —— h
led Miss —— into that slough just opposite your house
The fact was, in crossing the street, as they supposed, t
night being so very dark, they walked straight into th
slough that extended quite across the street and near
half way down the block; into it they went, until the
were nearly up to their waists in mud and water. Th
more they tried to extricate themselves, the deeper the
got into the mire; finally, at the suggestion of the la
whom I was accompanying, I told them to stand perfect
still until I could get a lantern, which I succeeded in doi
in a very short time, when I held the light up, so that v
could see them and they view themselves, you ought
have seen the look that girl gave me (in the meantin
the lady at my side had her mouth filled with linen ca
bric to keep from screaming right out), then, half laughi
and half crying, she paddled her own canoe until s
reached *terra firma*, then rushed for her home, which w
not more than fifty feet from them, nor had it been a
of the time, although they had been skirmishing in vario
directions. Meanwhile, the clerical gentleman had dra

himself out, covered with mud. Such a countenance!—it was a perfect black and tan; he shook himself, bade us good night, and left for his study. It may be of interest to some to know that the slough was located on Clark street, between Lake and South Water streets.

Many very amusing incidents occurred, which are worthy of recital, but a few more must suffice. One, I remember, was of a young lady crossing one of our principal streets, the way seemed clear, so she tripped along very gracefully until she had almost reached the opposite side, when the crust, which had formed from the heat of the sun, gave way, and down she began to go—down, down, down, until she had gone about as far down as she could, and was looking pitifully around for help from some source. A gentleman near by, observing her predicament, hastened to her rescue, and extricated the fair lady from her perilous position. You may be sure she was not as tidy when she again touched solid foundation as when she started to cross the street. Thanking the gentleman for his timely and polite assistance, she wended her way to the nearest convenient place, and, taking a forlorn look at herself, proceeded to adjust her *toilet*. The *finale* of this little incident was somewhat romantic, it furnished the means of culminating an acquaintance of friendship merely into one of admiration and affection, the result being that, not long after, the parties engaged in a matrimonial alliance, which was consummated in a remote part of the town, away from the thickly settled portion of the city—on the corner of Michigan avenue and Madison street. Their wedding tour was a drive to Hard Scrabble and back, a suburban retreat containing one log house, and situate about 4½ miles from town—the site now forming the outskirts of Bridgeport. The wedding *cortège* consisted of two dilapidated carriages and one buggy, all the available stylish turnouts that the city could boast of, except carts, and which, by the way, were the only means of conveyance for the *élite* of the town. A buffalo robe was placed in the bottom of the carts, they were backed up, received their precious freight, taken to their destination, and then dumped down like a load of coal.

Notwithstanding all these seeming inconveniences, there was more real social enjoyment in our pioneer society than

can now be found in the elegant and costly receptions
given in palatial mansions of wealth and refinement; there
was that absence of over-restraint; the strict forms of *eti-
quette* were not so closely observed; there were no million-
naires—no foreign Counts to entertain; no Parisian airs to
assume as a pre-requisite to initiation into the best society;
invitations were not sent on highly-perfumed Paris *billets
doux*, but by oral representation, thus: "George, if you see
James, tell him to invite Benjamin and William, and I
will invite Byron and Charles, to a little sociable to-night
at Maria's (now everybody knew Maria as well as Mrs.
Josiah Allen knew Betsy Bobbitt); you bring Andelucia,
and I will see that Agnes, Angeline, Elizabeth, and Rose
are there. We shall have a first-rate time. Old George
White will be there with his fiddle," etc. Mind you, these
are no fictitious names, but veritable actors on the social
stage at the time, some of whom are now living, and, were
they present, would at once recognize the truth of what I
am repeating. The George White mentioned was black
as the raven wing of the night, and was caterer for all
first society people. One of the necessary requisites, however, for attending these social gatherings, was, if the party
was a new comer, did he belong to the first society? If
yea, that was all that was required of him as a passport
to our social circle, otherwise no intercourse was enjoyed
until initiated into the first. You will observe, then, that
certain requisites were necessary before even the nabobs
of the east could enjoy these primitive receptions, unless
properly vouched for.

An amusing incident of the olden time, although not
reflecting favorably upon the morals of some of the members of our early associates, nevertheless, shows to what
abandon a few of our most prominent citizens would submit
themselves under a want of proper restraint. Two prominent legal gentlemen had left their office, and, passing the
old Tremont House, then located on the north-west corner
of Lake and Dearborn streets, they heard an unusual noise
in the dining-room. With much difficulty they succeeded
in gaining admission, and found five or six gentlemen of
the highest respectability having, what they were pleased
to call, "a high old time." One was rolling and kicking
up his heels on the dining table, divested of his coat and

vest, and making the welkin ring with his unearthly noise; another was at the lower end of the room *praying:* a third was dancing a war dance, with two Indians, around the dining table; a fourth, amusing himself by cutting up capers in imitation of an old-fashioned jig, all on his own responsibility; two others were lying fast asleep under the table. Thus they were all employed when these gentlemen gained an admittance. Finding escape by the doorway impossible, they took the next best plan, and jumped out the window. They were fined $5 each for their intrusion, by the parties having the "gay old time," which they promptly paid. We could give the names of all these parties, but they have passed away, and out of respect to the departed, we will refrain from so doing. We would say, however, that they all became honored members of society, filling City, State, and Federal offices of trust and responsibility with fidelity to the government and honor to themselves.

In migrating to a new country, many interesting circumstances occur, which leave a lasting impression upon the mind, notwithstanding intervening events that would be calculated to occupy the popular attention. I recall just now, among others, the Indian payments, which, I think, occurred as late as 1835 (a few tribes remained later, but not many). Their manner of giving in the number of each household, in order to receive their annuity, was in keeping with their own originality. Selecting one of the more prominent of their number (generally the chief) to receive their payment, the "*modus operandi*" was in this wise: for the heads of the family, two large notches were cut at the top of the stick, then smaller notches followed underneath, indicating the number of children in each family. Curiosity led me to inquire of Col. Boyd, the Indian Agent, if he was not occasionally imposed upon, or did they not sometimes make mistakes. He informed me that he had never detected an instance of fraud or mistake in the count during all the payments he had made. After receiving their payment, which was always in silver half dollars, they would at once repair to their wigwams and pass the money over to their squaws for safe-keeping, who would tie it up in one corner of their blankets, often to be removed by some adroit thief, who would lie in wait until they went to sleep, then cut it from the blanket; thus depriving the poor, ignorant creatures of all their worldly wealth, no one interesting themselves in their behalf, or sympathizing with them in their loss.

After their payment, many of them would remain several days, and favor us with a display of some of their principal amusements, such as shooting pennies, with bow and arrow, from a stick placed some distance from them in the road. They also performed a variety of dances, some of them exceedingly novel, particularly the sick dance. The sick person is placed at the entrance of the wigwam; one of their number takes his position just in front, with an instrument resembling a gong or tambourine; the relatives and friends of the invalid form a circle around the musician, all being gaily dressed and painted, each one holding in his hand the skin of some animal, generally an otter or mink; then, at the tap of the gong, and there is no mistaking the tap, for it is given with the full strength of the Indian, they all commence dancing around, singing, crying, and making other hideous noises; at a given signal bow before the patient and push out these perfumed skins toward them, after the manner of shaking incense. This dance continues at intervals until the sufferer either recovers or dies, but they generally die, for the noise is so intolerably great that it is next to impossible for them to recover. Their war dances, too, are very unique, differing entirely from the sick or peace dances, if possible, more noisy than either; but enough. On some future occasion, I may have the honor of presenting to you a more extended description of the social and religious doings in the earlier history of our beautiful city, and enter more into details respecting those who have gone to their rest, but who, while living, contributed so much toward the intellectual, historical, and social advancement of our present highly-refined Chicago Society.

CHICAGO IN 1836.

"STRANGE EARLY DAYS."

By HARRIET MARTINEAU.*

Author of "Society in America."

We had already met with some delays; and there was no seeing the end of the present adventure. There was some doubt whether we should not have done better to cross the southern end of Lake Michigan, from Niles to Chicago, by a little steam-boat, the Delaware, which was to leave Niles a few hours after our stage. It had been thought of at Niles; but there was some uncertainty about the departure of the boat; and we all anxiously desired to skirt the extremity of this great inland sea, and to see the new settlements on its shores. Had we done right in incurring this risk of detention? Right or wrong, here we were; and here we must wait upon events.

Our sleep, amidst the luxury of cleanliness and hospitality, was most refreshing. The next morning it was still raining, but less vehemently. After breakfast, we ladies employed ourselves in sweeping and dusting our room, and making the beds; as we had given our kind hostess too much trouble already. Then there was a Michigan City newspaper to be read; and I sat down to write letters. Before long, a wagon and four drove up to the door, the driver of which cried out that if there was any getting to Michigan City, he was our man. We equipped ourselves in our warmest and thickest clothing, put on our india-rubber shoes, packed ourselves and our luggage in the wagon, put up our umbrellas, and wondered what was to be our fate. When it had come to saying farewell, our hostess put her hands on my shoulders, kissed me on each cheek, and

---

* Died June 27, 1876, aged 77 years, at Ambleside, England.

3

said she had hoped for the pleasure of our company for another day. For my own part, I would willingly take her at her word, if my destiny should ever carry me near the great lakes again.

We jolted on for two miles and a-half through the woods, admiring the scarlet lilies, and the pink and white moccasin flower, which was brilliant. Then we arrived at the place of the vanished bridge. Our first prospect was of being paddled over, one by one, in the smallest of boats. But, when the capabilities of the place were examined, it was decided that we should wait in a house on the hill, while the neighbors, the passengers of the mail-stage, and the drivers, build a bridge. We waited patiently for nearly three hours, watching the busy men going in and out, gathering tidings of the freshet, and its effects, and being pleased to see how affectionate the woman of the house was to her husband, while she was cross to everybody else. It must have been vexatious to her to have her floor made wet and dirty, and all her household operations disturbed by a dozen strangers whom she had never invited. She let us have some dough-nuts, and gave us a gracious glance or two at parting.

We learned that a gentleman who followed us from Niles the preceding day, found the water nine feet deep, and was near drowning his horses, in a place which we had crossed without difficulty. This very morning, a bridge which we had proved and passed, gave way with the stage, and the horses had to be dug and rolled out of the mud, when they were on the point of suffocation. Such a freshet had never been known to the present inhabitants.

At half-past two, the bridge was announced complete, and we re-entered our wagon, to lead the cavalcade across it, slowly, anxiously, with a man at the head of each leader, we entered the water, and saw it rise to the nave of the wheels. Instead of jolting, as usual, we mounted and descended each log individually. The mail-wagon followed, with two or three horsemen. There was also a singularly benevolent personage, who jumped from the other wagon, and waded through all the doubtful places, to prove them. He leaped and splashed through the water, which was sometimes up to his waist, as if it was the most agreeable sport in the world. In one of these gullies, the forepart of our wagon sank and stuck, so as to throw us forward, and make it doubtful in what mode we should emerge from the water. Then the rim of one of the wheels was found to be loose; and the whole cavalcade stopped till it was mended. I never could understand how wagons were made in the back-country; they seemed to be elastic, from the shocks and twisting they would bear without giving way. To form an accurate idea of what they have to bear, a traveller should sit on a seat without springs, placed between the hind wheels, and thus proceed on a corduroy road. The effect is less fatiguing and more amusing, of riding in a wagon whose seats are on springs, while the vehicle itself is not. In that case, the feet are dancing an involuntary jig, all the way; while the rest of the body is in a state of entire repose.

The drive was so exciting and pleasant, the rain having ceased, that I was taken by surprise by our arrival at Michigan City. The driver announced our approach by a series of flourishes on one note of his common horn, which made the most ludicrous music I ever listened to.

We were anxious to see the mighty fresh water sea. We made inquiry in the piazza; and a sandy hill, close by, covered with the pea-vine, was pointed out to us. We ran up it, and there beheld what we had come so far to see. There it was, deep, green, and swelling on the horizon, and whitening into a broad and heavy surf as it rolled in towards the shore. Hence, too, we could make out the geography of the city. The whole scene stands insulated in my memory, as absolutely singular; and, at this distance of time, scarcely credible. I was so well aware on the spot that it would be so, that I made careful and copious notes of what I saw: but memoranda have nothing to do with such emotions as were caused by the sight of that enormous body of tumultuous waters, rolling in apparently upon the helpless forest,—everywhere else so majestic.

Immediately after supper we went out for a walk, which, in peculiarity, comes next to that in the Mammoth Cave; if, indeed, it be second to it. The scene was like what I had always fancied the Norway coast, but for the wild flowers, which grew among the pines on the slope, almost into the tide. I longed to spend an entire day on this flowery and shadowy margin of the inland sea. I plucked handfuls of pea-vine and other trailing flowers, which seemed to run all over the ground. We found on the

sands an army, like Pharaoh's drowned host, of disabled
butterflies, beetles, and flies of the richest colors and lustre,
driven over the lake by the storm. Charley* found a small
turtle alive. An elegant little schooner, "the Sea Serpent
of Chicago," was stranded, and formed a beautiful object
as she lay dark between the sand and the surf. The sun
was going down. We watched the sunset, not remember-
ing that the refraction above the fresh waters would probably cause some remarkable appearance. We looked at
one another in amazement at what we saw. First, there
were three gay, inverted rainbows between the water and
the sun, then hidden behind a little streak of cloud. Then
the sun emerged from behind this only cloud, urn-shaped;
a glistering golden urn. Then it changed, rather suddenly,
to an enormous golden acorn. Then to a precise resem-
blance, except being prodigiously magnified, of Saturn with
his ring. This was the most beautiful apparition of all.
Then it was quickly narrowed and elongated till it was like
the shaft of a golden pillar; and thus it went down square.
Long after its disappearance, a lustrous, deep crimson
dome, seemingly solid, rested steadily on the heaving
waters. An inexperienced navigator might be pardoned
for making all sail towards it; it looked so real.

On our road to Chicago, the next day,—a road winding
in and out among the sand-hills, we were called to alight,
and run up a bank to see a wreck. It was the wreck of
the Delaware;—the steamer in which it had been a question whether we should not proceed from Niles to Chicago.
She had a singular twist in her middle, where she was
nearly broken in two. Her passengers stood up to the
neck in water, for twenty-four hours before they were taken
off; a worse inconvenience than any that we had suffered
by coming the other way. The first thing the passengers
from the Delaware did, when they had dried and warmed
themselves on shore, was to sign a letter to the captain,
which appeared in all the neighboring newspapers, thanking him for the great comfort they had enjoyed on board
his vessel. It is to be presumed that they meant previously
to their having to stand up to their necks in water.

In the wood which borders the prairie on which Chicago
stands, we saw an encampment of United States' troops.
Since the rising of the Creeks in Georgia, some months

* Son of Rev. Dr. Follen.

before, there had been apprehensions of an Indian war
along the whole frontier. It was believed that a corre-
spondence had taken place among all the tribes, from the
Cumaches, who were engaged to fight for the Mexicans in
Texas, up to the northern tribes among whom we were
going. It was believed that the war-belt was circulating
among the Winnebagoes, the warlike tribe who inhabit the
western shores of Lake Michigan; and the government had
sent troops to Chicago, to keep them in awe. It was of
some consequence to us to ascertain the real state of the
case; and we were glad to find that alarm was subsiding so
fast, that the troops were soon allowed to go where they
were more wanted. As soon as they had recovered from
the storm, which seemed to have incommoded everybody,
they broke up their encampment, and departed.

Chicago looks raw and bare, standing on the high prairie
above the lake shore. The houses appear all insignificant,
and run up in various directions, without any principle at
all. A friend of mine who resides there had told me that
we should find the inns intolerable, at the period of the
great land sales, which bring a concourse of speculators to
the place. It was even so. The very sight of them was
intolerable; and there was not room for our party among
them all. I do not know what we should have done,
(unless to betake ourselves to the vessels in the harbor,) if
our coming had not been foreknown, and most kindly provided for. We were divided between three families, who
had the art of removing all our scruples about intrud-
ing on perfect strangers. None of us will lose the lively
and pleasant associations with the place, which were caused
by the hospitalities of its inhabitants.

I never saw a busier place than Chicago was at the time
of our arrival. The streets were crowded with land speculators, hurrying from one sale to another. A negro, dressed
up in scarlet, bearing a scarlet flag, and riding a white
horse with housings of scarlet, announced the times of sale.
At every street corner where he stopped, the crowed flocked
round him; and it seemed as if some prevalent mania infected the whole people. The rage for speculation might
fairly be so regarded. As the gentlemen of our party
walked the streets, store-keepers hailed them from their
doors, with offers of farms, and all manner of land-lots, ad-
vising them to speculate before the price of land rose

higher. A young lawyer, of my acquaintance there,* had realized five hundred dollars per day, the five preceding days, by merely making out titles to land. Another friend had realized, in two years, ten times as much money as he had before fixed upon as a competence for life. Of course, this rapid money-making is a merely temporary evil. A bursting of the bubble must come soon. The absurdity of the speculation is so striking, that the wonder is that the fever should have attained such a height as I witnessed. The immediate occasion of the bustle which prevailed, the week we were at Chicago, was the sale of lots, to the value of two millions of dollars, along the course of a projected canal; and of another set, immediately behind these. Persons not intending to game, and not infected with mania, would endeavor to form some reasonable conjecture as to the ultimate value of the lots, by calculating the cost of the canal, the risks from accident, from the possible competition from other places, etc., and, finally, the possible profits, under the most favorable circumstance, within so many years' purchase. Such a calculation would serve as some sort of guide as to the amount of purchase-money to be risked. Whereas, wild land on the banks of a canal, not yet even marked out, was selling at Chicago for more than rich land, well improved, in the finest part of the valley of the Mohawk, on the banks of a canal which is already the medium of an almost inestimable amount of traffic. If sharpers and gamblers were to be the sufferers by the impending crash at Chicago, no one would feel much concerned: but they, unfortunately, are the people who encourage the delusion, in order to profit by it. Many a high-spirited, but unexperienced, young man; many a simple settler, will be ruined for the advantage of knaves.

Others, besides lawyers and speculators by trade, make a fortune in such extraordinary times. A poor man at Chicago had a pre-emption right to some land, for which he paid in the morning one hundred and fifty dollars. In the afternoon, he sold it to a friend of mine for five thousand dollars. A poor Frenchman,† married to a squaw, had a suit pending, when I was there, which he was likely to gain, for the right of purchasing some land by the lake for one hundred dollars, which would immediately become worth one million dollars.

* Joseph N. Balestier, Esq., now of Brattleboro, Vt   † Gen. John B. Beaubien.

There was much gaiety going on at Chicago, as well as business. On the evening of our arrival a fancy fair took place. As I was too much fatigued to go, the ladies sent me a bouquet of prairie flowers. There is some allowable pride in the place about its society. It is a remarkable thing to meet such an assemblage of educated, refined, and wealthy persons as may be found there, living in small, inconvenient houses on the edge of a wild prairie. There is a mixture, of course. I heard of a family of half-breeds setting up a carriage, and wear fine jewellery. When the present intoxication of prosperity passes away, some of the inhabitants will go back to the eastward; there will be an accession of settlers from the mechanic classes; good houses will have been built for the richer families, and the singularity of the place will subside. It will be like all the other new and thriving lake and river ports of America. Meantime, I am glad to have seen it in its strange early days.

We dined one day with a gentleman* who had been Indian agent among the Winnebagoes for some years. He and his lady seem to have had the art of making themselves as absolutely Indian in their sympathies and manners as the welfare of the savages among whom they lived required. They were the only persons I met with who, really knowing the Indians, had any regard for them. The testimony was universal to the good faith, and other virtues of savage life of the unsophisticated Indians; but they were spoken of in a tone of dislike, as well as pity, by all but this family; and they certainly had studied their Indian neighbors very thoroughly. The ladies of Indian agents ought to be women of nerve. Our hostess had slept for weeks with a loaded pistol on each side her pillow, and a dagger under it, when expecting an attack from a hostile tribe.† The foe did not, however, come nearer than within a few miles. Her husband's sister‡ was in the massacre when the fort was abandoned, in 1812. Her father and her husband were in the battle, and her mother and young brothers and sisters sat in a boat on the lake near. Out of seventy whites, only seventeen escaped, among whom were her family. She was wounded in the ankle, as she sat on her horse. A painted

John H. Kinzie, Esq.   † At Fort Winnebago, 1832.
‡ Mrs. Helm, now Mrs. Geo. C. Bates, Salt Lake City.

Indian, in warlike costume, came leaping up to her, and seized her horse, as she supposed, to murder her. She fought him vigorously, and he bore it without doing her any injury. He spoke, but she could not understand him. Another frightful savage came up, and the two led her horse to the lake, and into it, in spite of her resistance, till the water reached their chins. She concluded that they meant to drown her; but they contented themselves with holding her on her horse till the massacre was over, when they led her out in safety. They were friendly Indians, sent by her husband to guard her. She could not but admire their patience, when she found how she had been treating her protectors.

We had the fearful pleasure of seeing various savage dances: performed by the Indian agent and his brother,* with the accompaniments of complete costume, barbaric music, and whooping. The most intelligible to us was the Discovery Dance, a highly descriptive pantomime. We saw the Indian go out armed for war. We saw him reconnoitre, make signs to his comrades, sleep, warm himself, load his rifle, sharpen his scalping-knife, steal through the grass within rifle-shot of his foes, fire, scalp one of them, and dance, whooping, and triumphing. There was a dreadful truth about the whole, and it made our blood run cold. It realized hatred and horror as effectually as Taglioni does love and grace.

We were unexpectedly detained over the Sunday at Chicago; and Dr. F.† was requested to preach. Though only two hours' notice was given, a respectable congregation was assembled in the large room of the Lake House; a new hotel then building. Our seats were a few chairs and benches, and planks laid on trestles. The preacher stood behind a rough pine-table, on which a large Bible was placed. I was never present at a more interesting service; and I know that there were others who felt with me.

From Chicago, we made an excursion into the prairies. Our young lawyer-friend threw behind him the five hundred dollars per day, which he was making, and went with us. I thought him wise; for there is that to be had in the wilderness which money cannot buy. We drove out of the town at ten o'clock in the morning, too late by two hours; but it was impossible to overcome the introductions to

* John H. and Robert A. Kinzie.   † Rev. Dr. Follen.

strangers, and the bustle of our preparations, any sooner. Our party consisted of seven, besides the driver. Our vehicle was a wagon with four horses.

We had first to cross the prairie, nine miles wide, on the lake edge of which Chicago stands. This prairie is not usually wet so early in the year; but at this time the water stood almost up to the nave of the wheels: and we crossed it at a walking pace. I saw here, for the first time in the United States, the American primrose. It grew in profusion over the whole prairie, as far as I could see; not so large and fine as in English green-houses, but graceful and pretty. I now found the truth of what I had read about the difficulty of distinguishing distances on a prairie. The feeling is quite bewildering. A man walking near looks like a Goliath a mile off. I mistook a covered wagon without horses, at a distance of fifty yards, for a white house near the horizon: and so on. We were not sorry to reach the belt of trees, which bounded the swamp we had passed. At a house here, where we stopped to water the horses, and eat dough-nuts, we saw a crowd of emigrants; which showed that we had not yet reached the bounds of civilization. A little further on we came to the river Aux Plaines, spelled on a sign board "Oplain." The ferry here is a monopoly, and the public suffers accordingly. There is only one small flat boat for the service of the concourse of people now pouring into the prairies. Though we happened to arrive nearly first of the crowd of to-day, we were detained on the bank above an hour; and then our horses went over at two crossings, and the wagon and ourselves at the third. It was a pretty scene, if we had not been in a hurry; the country wagons and teams in the wood by the side of the quiet clear river; and the oxen swimming over, yoked, with only their patient faces visible above the surface. After crossing, we proceeded briskly till we reached a single house, where, or nowhere, we were to dine. The kind hostess bestirred herself to provide us a good dinner of tea, bread, ham, potatoes, and strawberries, of which a whole pailful, ripe and sweet, had been gathered by the children in the grass round the house, within one hour. While dinner was preparing, we amused ourselves with looking over an excellent small collection of books, belonging to Miss Cynthia, the daughter of the hostess.

I never saw insulation. (not desolation,) to compare with

the situation of a settler on a wide prairie. A single house in the middle of Salisbury Plain would be desolate. A single house on a prairie has clumps of trees near it, rich fields about it; and flowers, strawberries, and running water at hand. But when I saw a settler's child tripping out of home-bounds, I had a feeling that it would never get back again. It looked like putting out into Lake Michigan in a canoe. The soil round the dwellings is very rich. It makes no dust, it is so entirely vegetable. It requires merely to be once turned over to produce largely; and, at present, it appears to be inexhaustible. As we proceeded, the scenery became more and more like what all travellers compare it to,—a boundless English park. The grass was wilder, the occasional footpath not so trim, and the single trees less majestic; but no park ever displayed anything equal to the grouping of the trees within the windings of the blue, brimming river Aux Plaines.

We had met with so many delays that we felt doubts about reaching the place where we had intended to spend the night. At sunset, we found ourselves still nine miles from Joliet;* but we were told that the road was good, except a small "slew" or two; and there was half a moon shining behind a thin veil of clouds; so we pushed on. We seemed latterly to be travelling on a terrace overlooking a wide champaign, where a dark waving line might indicate the winding of the river, between its clumpy banks. Our driver descended, and went forward, two or three times, to make sure of our road; and, at length, we rattled down a steep descent, and found ourselves among houses. This was not our resting-place, however. The Joliet hotel lay on the other side of the river. We were directed to a foot-bridge by which we were to pass; and a ford below for the wagon. We strained our eyes in vain for the foot-bridge; and our gentlemen peeped and pryed about for some time. All was still but the rippling river, and everybody asleep in the houses that were scattered about. We ladies were presently summoned to put on our water-proof shoes, and alight. A man showed himself who had risen

* I preserve the original name, which is that of the first French missionary who visited these parts. The place is now commonly called Juliet; and a settlement near has actually been named Romeo: so that I fear there is little hope of a restoration of the honorable primitive name.

from his bed to help us in our need. The foot-bridge consisted, for some way, of two planks, with a hand-rail on
one side: but, when we were about a-third of the way over,
one-half of the planks, and the hand-rail had disappeared.
We actually had to cross the rushing, deep river on a line
of single planks, by dim moonlight, at past eleven at night.
The great anxiety was about Charley; but between his
father and the guide, he managed very well. This guide
would accept nothing but thanks. He "did not calculate
to take any pay." Then we waited some time for the
wagon to come up from the ford. I suspected it had
passed the spot where we stood, and had proceeded to the
village, where we saw a twinkling light, now disappearing,
and now re-appearing. It was so, and the driver came
back to look for us, and tell us that the light we saw was a
signal from the hotel-keeper, whom we found, standing on
his door-step, and sheltering his candle with his hand. We
sat down and drank milk in the bar, while he went to con-
sult with his wife what was to be done with us, as every
bed in the house was occupied. We, meanwhile, agreed
that the time was now come for us to enjoy an adventure
which we had often anticipated: sleeping in a barn. We
had all declared ourselves anxious to sleep in a barn, if we
could meet with one that was air-tight, and well supplied
with hay. Such a barn was actually on these premises.
We were prevented, however, from all practising the freak
by the prompt hospitality of our hostess. Before we knew
what she was about, she had risen and dressed herself, put
clean sheets on her own bed, and made up two others on
the floor of the same room; so that the ladies and Charley
were luxuriously accommodated. Two sleepy personages
crawled down stairs to offer their beds to our gentlemen.
Mr. L.* and our Chicago friend, however, persisted in sleeping in the barn. Next morning, we all gave a very gratify-
ing report of our lodgings. When we made our acknowl-
edgments to our hostess, she said she thought that people
who could go to bed quietly every night ought to be ready
to give up to tired travellers. Whenever she travels, I
hope she will be treated as she treated us. She let us have
breakfast as early as half-past five, the next morning, and
gave Charley a bun at parting, lest he should be too hungry
before we could dine.

* Ellis Gray Loring, Esq.

The great object of our expedition, Mount Joliet, was two miles distant from this place. We had to visit it, and perform the journey back to Chicago, forty miles, before night. The mount is only sixty feet high; yet it commands a view which I shall not attempt to describe, either in its vastness, or its soft beauty. The very spirit of tranquility resides in this paradisy scene. The next painter who would worthily illustrate Milton's Morning Hymn, should come and paint what he sees from Mount Joliet, on a dewy summer's morning, when a few light clouds are gently sailing in the sky, and their shadows traversing the prairie. I thought I had never seen green levels till now; and only among mountains had I before known the beauty of wandering showers. Mount Joliet has the appearance of being an artificial mound, its sides are so uniformly steep, and its form so regular. Its declivity was bristling with flowers; among which were conspicuous the scarlet lily, the white convolvulus, and a tall, red flower of the scabia form. We disturbed a night-hawk, sitting on her eggs, on the ground. She wheeled round and round over our heads, and, I hope, returned to her eggs before they were cold.

Not far from the mount was a log-house, where the rest of the party went in to dry their feet, after having stood long in the wet grass. I remained outside, watching the light showers, shifting in the partial sunlight from clump to level, and from reach to reach of the brimming and winding river. The nine miles of prairie, which we had traversed in dim moonlight last night, were now exquisitely beautiful, as the sun shone fitfully upon them.

We saw a prairie wolf, very like a yellow dog, trotting across our path, this afternoon. Our hostess of the preceding day, expecting us, had an excellent dinner ready for us. We were detained a shorter time at the ferry, and reached the belt of trees at the edge of Nine-mile Prairie, before sunset. Here, in common prudence, we ought to have stopped till the next day, even if no other accommodation could be afforded us than a roof over our heads. We deserved an ague for crossing the swamp after dark, in an open wagon, at a foot pace. Nobody was aware of this in time, and we set forward; the feet of our wearied horses plashing in water at every step of the nine miles. There was no road; and we had to trust to the instinct of driver

and horses to keep us in the right direction.   I rather think
the driver attempted to amuse himself by exciting our fears.
He hinted more than once at the difficulty of finding the
way; at the improbability that we should reach Chicago
before midnight; and at the danger of our wandering about
the marsh all night, and finding ourselves at the opposite
edge of the prairie in the morning.   Charley was bruised
and tired.   All the rest were hungry and cold.   It was
very dreary.   The driver bade us look to our right hand.
A black bear was trotting alongside of us, at a little distance.   After keeping up his trot for some time, he turned
off from our track.   The sight of him made up for all,—
even if ague should follow, which I verily believe it would.
But we escaped all illness.   It is remarkable that I never
saw ague but once.   The single case that I met with was
in autumn, at the Falls of Niagara.

    I had promised Dr. F. a long story about English poli-
tics, when a convenient opportunity should occur.   I
thought the present an admirable one; for nobody seemed
to have anything to say, and it was highly desirable that
something should be said.   I made my story long enough
to beguile four miles: by which time, some were too tired,
and others too much disheartened, for more conversation.
Something white was soon after visible.   Our driver gave
out that it was a house, half a mile from Chicago.   But no:
it was an emigrant encampment, on a morsel of raised, dry
ground; and again we were uncertain whether we were in
the right road.   Presently, however, the Chicago beacon
was visible, shining a welcome to us through the dim, misty
air.   The horses seemed to see it, for they quickened their
pace; and before half-past ten, we were on the bridge.

    The family, at my temporary home, were gone up to
their chambers; but the wood-fire was soon replenished,
tea made, and the conversation growing lively.   My companions were received as readily at their several resting-
places.   When we next met, we found ourselves all dis-
posed to place warm hospitality very high on the list of
virtues.

    While we were at Detroit, we were most strongly urged
to return thither by the Lakes, instead of by either of the
Michigan roads.   From place to place, in my previous
travelling, I had been told of the charms of the Lakes, and
especially of the Island of Mackinaw.   Every officer's lady

who has been in garrison there, is eloquent upon the delights of Mackinaw. As our whole party, however, could
not spare time to make so wide a circuit, we had not intended to indulge ourselves with a further variation in our
travels than to take the upper road back to Detroit; having
left it by the lower. On Sunday, June 27, news arrived at
Chicago that this upper road had been rendered impassable
by the rains. A sailing ship,* the only one on the Lakes,
and now on her first trip, was to leave Chicago for Detroit
and Buffalo, the next day. The case was clear: the party
must divide. Those who were obliged to hasten home
must return by the road we came: the rest must proceed
by water. On Charley's account the change of plan was
desirable; as the heats were beginning to be so oppressive
as to render travelling in open wagons unsafe for a child.
It was painful to break up our party at the extreme point of
our journey; but it was clearly right. So Mr. and Mrs. L.
took their chance by land; and the rest of us went on
board the Milwaukee, at two o'clock on the afternoon of
the 28th.

Mrs. F. and I were the only ladies on board; and there
was no stewardess. The steward was obliging. and the
ladies' cabin was clean and capacious; and we took possession of it with a feeling of comfort. Our pleasant impres-
sions, however, were not of long duration. The vessel was
crowed with persons who had come to the land sales at
Chicago, and were taking their passage back to Milwaukee;
a settlement on the western shore of the lake, about eighty
miles from Chicago. Till we should reach Milwaukee, we
could have the ladies' cabin only during a part of the day.
I say a part of the day, because some of the gentry did not
leave our cabin till near nine in the morning; and others
chose to come down, and go to bed, as early as seven in
the evening, without troubling themselves to give us five
minutes' notice, or to wait till we could put up our needles,
or wipe our pens. This ship was the only place in America where I saw a prevalence of bad manners. It was the
place of all others to select for the study of such; and no
reasonable person would look for anything better among
land-speculators, and settlers in regions so new as to be
almost without women. None of us had ever before seen,
in America, a disregard of women. The swearing was

* Ship Milwaukee.

incessant; and the spitting such as to amaze my American companions as much as myself.

Supper was announced presently after we had sailed; and when we came to the table, it was full, and no one offered to stir, to make room for us. The captain, who was very careful of our comfort, arranged that we should be better served henceforth; and no difficulty afterwards occurred. At dinner, the next day, we had a specimen of how such personage as we had on board are managed on an emergency. The captain gave notice, from the head of the table, that he did not choose our party to be intruded on in the cabin; and that any one who did not behave with civility at table should be turned out. He spoke with decision and good-humor; and the effect was remarkable. Everything on the table was handed to us; and no more of the gentry came down into our cabin to smoke, or throw themselves on the cushions to sleep, while we sat at work. Our fare was what might be expected on Lake Michigan. Salt beef and pork, and sea-biscuit; tea without milk, bread, and potatoes. Charley throve upon potatoes and bread; and we all had the best results of food,—health and strength.

A little schooner which left Chicago at the same time with ourselves, and reached Milwaukee first, was a pretty object. On the 29th, we were only twenty-five miles from the settlement; but the wind was so unfavorable that it was doubtful whether we should reach it that day. Some of the passengers amused themselves by gaming, down in the hold; others by parodying a methodist sermon, and singing a mock hymn. We did not get rid of them till noon on the 30th, when we had the pleasure of seeing our ship disgorge twenty-five into one boat, and two into another. The atmosphere was so transparent as to make the whole scene appear as if viewed through an opera-glass; the still, green waters, the dark boats with their busy oars, the moving passengers, and the struggles of one to recover his hat, which had fallen overboard. We were yet five miles from Milwaukee; but we could see the bright, wooded coast, with a few white dots of houses.

While Dr. F. went on shore, to see what was to be seen, we had the cabin cleaned out, and took, once more, complete possession of it, for both day and night. As soon as this was done, seven young women came down the com-

panion-way, seated themselves round the cabin, and began
to question us. They were the total female population of
Milwaukee; which settlement now contains four hundred
souls. We were glad to see these ladies; for it was natural enough that the seven women should wish to behold
two more, when such a chance offered. A gentleman of
the place, who came on board this afternoon, told me that
a printing-press had arrived a few hours before; and that a
newspaper would speedily appear.* He was kind enough
to forward the first number to me a few weeks afterwards;
and I was amused to see how pathetic an appeal to the
ladies of more thickly-settled districts it contained; implor-
ing them to cast a favorable eye on Milwaukee, and its
hundreds of bachelors. Milwaukee had been settled since
the preceding November. It had good stores; (to judge
by the nature and quantity of goods sent ashore from our
ship); it had a printing-press and newspaper, before the
settlers had had time to get wives. I heard these new settlement sometimes called "patriarchal:" but what would
the patriarchs have said to such an order of affairs?

Dr. F. returned from the town with apple-pies, cheese,
and ale, wherewith to vary our ship diet. With him arrived such a number of towns-people, that the steward
wanted to turn us out of our cabin once more: but we were
sturdy, appealed to the captain, and were confirmed in possession. From this time, began the delights of our voyage.
The moon, with her long train of glory, was magnificent
to-night: the vast body of water on which she shone being
as calm as if the winds were dead.

The navigation of these lakes, is at present, a mystery.
They have not yet been properly surveyed. Our captain
had gone to and fro on Lake Huron, but had never before
been on Lake Michigan; and this was rather an anxious
voyage to him. We had got aground on the sand-bar
before Milwaukee harbor; and on the 1st of July, all hands
were busy in unshipping the cargo, to lighten the vessel,
instead of carrying her up to the town. An elegant little
schooner was riding at anchor near us; and we were well
amused in admiring her, and in watching the bustle on
deck, till some New England youths, and our Milwaukee
acquaintance, brought us, from the shore, two newspapers,
some pebbles, flowers, and a pitcher of fine strawberries.

* Milwaukee Sentinel,

www.ingramcontent.com/pod-product-compliance
Lightning Source LLC
Chambersburg PA
CBHW021555270326
41931CB00009B/1221